Blokes and Birds

Blokes
and
Birds

Edited by **STEPHEN MOSS**

Foreword by **BILL ODDIE**

NEW HOLLAND

CONTENTS

FOREWORD BY BILL ODDIE

Blokes and Birds! Oh please! I must admit I never thought the day would come when my name would be associated with such a distasteful title.

Have I not campaigned most of my life against gratuitous 'bird' jokes? You know the sort of thing, "I'm a bird watcher too. Know what I mean? Eh? Eh? The two-legged kind."

To which my response has always been:

"No, I don't know what you mean. And all birds have two legs, actually. Unless they've lost one. In which case, do you really think it is clever or smart to laugh at crippled wildlife?"

I have never yet met a woman or girl who was flattered to be called a 'bird'. (Mind you, I can't think why not, since birds are the most gorgeous creatures on earth.)

Neither would I, personally, wish to be referred to as a 'bloke'. What does it mean, anyway? A real man? No, a beer-swilling, foul-mouthed, sexist yobbo, more like. I am proud to say that I have never considered myself to be a 'bloke' and I assure you I will never become one.

And nor would any of my friends – or so I thought. Imagine my disgust and disappointment, therefore, when I discovered that several people I know – and like – have actually contributed to this book. Good grief, my producer at the BBC Natural History Unit, Stephen Moss, has even allowed his name to be put on the front cover! What's more – to add insult to injury – I am utterly mortified to see that I am myself named, and therefore implicated in at least two of these supposedly gripping tales. Well, I can't do much about that, because the stories are true (and quite amusing actually).

Nevertheless, I do hereby completely disassociate myself from this dastardly collection...even if it is rather a good read!

Swallow: a cheeky-faced miracle of migration.

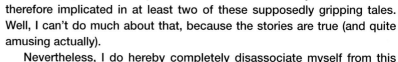

INTRODUCTION

Why is birdwatching an essentially male hobby? For despite a welcome increase in the number of female birders, the majority of serious birdwatchers are still men.

Is it because we men evolved as hunters, and, now that there's no need to kill our food to live, we seek out birds instead? Does it pander to the very masculine urge to make lists – 'organic trainspotting' – as one unkind observer suggested? Or is it, like appreciating music or art, something that fulfils a basic human instinct to take an interest in the world about us? Perhaps it is all of these things – and more. To quote one of the founders of modern birding, the late James Fisher:

> *"The observation of birds may be a superstition, a tradition, an art, a science, a pleasure, a hobby, or a bore; this depends entirely on the nature of the observer."*

9

Above and Opposite: *The Isles of Scilly are the ultimate autumn destination for hundreds of Britain's twitchers – keen birders whose main aim is to see rare birds. The crowd* **opposite** *are searching for a skulking bird while the miserable bunch* **above** *are heading for a rainstorm and one of the outlying islands.*

Above: *Some birders combine their hobby with a profession – like*
wildlife recordist Chris Watson.

Whatever the reason, more and more men are being bitten by the birding bug. It starts as a casual interest and soon develops into a hobby, then an obsession, and finally a consuming passion which invariably lasts for the rest of their life. Not that birders are so single-minded that they ignore everything else, but they do inhabit a parallel universe, in which they look at the world in a very different way from their fellow human beings. For a birder doesn't just look out of a car window and see people, traffic and signs for the local fast-food takeaway. Rather, he watches for that tell-tale movement that signifies the appearance of a bird; then instantly – and instinctively – puts a name to it. Identification is the key to the birding experience, for how can you appreciate something if you don't know what it is?

This doesn't just apply to what he sees. Sounds, too, take on a whole new dimension. For there are few places where you can't hear the songs and calls of birds. They wake us up on spring mornings and surprise us as we return home late in winter. They demand attention, and invariably get it – either with an identification muttered underneath our breath, or simply registered in our brain and filed away in that mental list of all the birds we have ever heard or seen.

Above: *Others, like photographer, David Tipling go to extremes in pursuit of birds.*

Whether a birder is sitting at home or driving down the motorway, in Britain or abroad, birds will demand attention. To tell a birder to ignore what he sees or hears is like telling a musician to block out a tune or forcing a sportsman not to catch a ball when you throw it at him.

To continue the sporting analogy, the book that reminds me most of the way birders inhabit a parallel universe is Nick Hornby's *Fever Pitch*, the tale of an obsessive Arsenal supporter. Both football fan and birder are in thrall to the changes of the seasons, which dictate their movements and preoccupations. Both experience joys and setbacks, thrills and boredom, passion and intense frustration. And just as the dedicated fan can remember every great goal and every missed penalty, so the keen birder can recall memorable sights, sounds and experiences going back years – sometimes even decades. Best of all, Hornby knows that when Arsenal win a cup final or league title, his friends and family will think of him; just as I know that when a rare bird is in the news, people I haven't seen for years will suddenly will remember my name, and wonder what I'm doing now.

It is easy to sneer at grown men being fascinated by a pastime somehow associated with childhood – a hobby, such as stamp-collecting, that they're supposed to have grown out of by the time they reach maturity. Another view is that a lifetime's interest – in football or birds, or indeed anything else – gives a continuity and meaning to our lives, one that seems to be lacking in today's secular world. Utimately, birding is just one of many activities that marks us as human, and separates us from the rest of God's creation.

Below: *With his company, C J Wildbird Foods, Chris Whittles is a leading entrepreneur of the bird world.*

Okay, so birding isn't a religion. Not even its keenest devotees would claim that. But it does put us in touch with nature at a deep, almost subconscious level; giving us a link with the rhythm of the seasons and with creatures whose lives intersect with our own.

Birding also brings a kind of cohesion to an increasingly fragmented society. Birders are part of a community of like-minded souls. A community that is not just confined to Britain – most birders have friends around the world, whose shared interest transcends national boundaries. *Blokes and Birds* contains 40 stories – some from close to home, others from far-flung places. Each tale conveys one aspect of why birders devote so much time, energy and effort to watching birds. Some are amusing, others deadly serious. In some, the writer experiences frustration, while in others he achieves a state of intense pleasure – a kind of birding nirvana. What they have in common is that they are told by people whose lives have been enhanced by their love of birds.

Above: *Stuart Winter's claim to fame is that he writes Britain's first tabloid birdwatching column.*

The stories are illustrated by leading bird photographer, Robin Chittenden, and each 'bloke' has chosen his favourite British bird and explained why it is special to him.

On a personal note, I love watching birds because they are something to get up for on cold winter mornings. They constantly surprise me with their behaviour and habits. They are some of the most beautiful creatures on the planet. I have travelled the world, and visited many places I would never have seen, were it not for birds. Some of my dearest friends are birders...and the love of birds led me to the love of my life, my wife, Suzanne.

So read on and by the time you finish this book you will finally understand why blokes are so obsessed with birds...

PLAYING HARD TO GET

Mark Andrews is a bird artist specializing in the avifauna of Africa, a continent which he has visited countless times. It took him nearly ten years to see the Picathartes, but he made it in the end.

I'm not sure where I first heard about Picathartes – or rockfowl, as it is often known. But in the early 1980s when I was working at Twycross Zoo, I found a photograph of a Picathartes and I just knew I had to see one.

In 1988, an opportunity arose with BirdLife International to help with a project in Cameroon, home of the rockfowl. I visited a traditional site, and found a guide who swore he knew the bird. "Dat beef like stony place," he informed me whilst studying the picture. Twenty four hours later, having been lost up lava flows, bewitched by voodoo and having roughed it overnight, we cut our way out, and he announced calmly that they were easier to find on the beach. I moved on.

Expeditions into Korup produced old nests and bad hangovers, the local 'boom-boom' brewed to maximum strength. Mount Kupe changed my life for, although I glimpsed the rockfowl, it wasn't enough. The mountain was so majestic, mysterious and fascinating, I vowed to come back. In 1990, I returned, and during the next three months we scoured the mountain, looking for the Picathartes.

We found old nests, surveyed darkened caves and descended valley bottoms and eventually, we found a site that looked active. Peering into the gloom, something moved, a willowy shape at the back of the cave. I moved away and waited to see what would come out.

A loud hiss from behind made my stomach churn I was sure I was about to be nailed by a viper. Turning to face my assailant I was confronted by an apparition. Not six feet away, sporting a fluorescent blue and red bonnet set off by a white moustache and a yellow belly, sat an inquisitive rockfowl, hissing. For a few minutes I faced him in awe before, like Zebedee, he sprang away.

Like the Picathartes, the Firecrest refuses to show itself easily, making a sighting a rewarding experience every time.

WHO DARES WINS

Tim Appleton is the co-founder of the British Birdwatching Fair. He developed the Rutland Water Nature Reserve and is currently the Reserve manager. He started the project for reintroducing breeding Ospreys to England and is vice-president of the British Ornithologists' Union.

On a birding trip to Tanzania, a change of planes at Addis Ababa involved a stopover of several hours, and the prospect of ticking off some Ethiopian birds. However, disappointment descended as we realized there were no windows in the transit lounge. But group member Bill Oddie found a small window in the Gent's lavatory that overlooked the airfield. We took it in turns to perch precariously on the edge of the toilet or on a fellow birder's shoulders. The airport officials became suspicious when they spotted women going into the Gents, and an armed guard ushered us back into the main building. We had, however clocked up several species including Wattled Ibis, a rare Ethiopian endemic!

While the others were having a coffee, Bill and I decided to have another go, and, attaching ourselves to a group leaving the departure lounge, and quickly started to add many more birds to our Ethiopian list. We could see, just beyond the airport fence, a tantalizing area of scrubland, which we longed to explore. We explained to a gullible guard that we had postcards in need of urgent posting, and to our surprise, were waved through. Once out of sight we whipped out our binoculars and birded in complete freedom.

Suddenly, a soldier ran towards us brandishing an AK47 rifle. We showed him our field guide by way of an explanation, but it didn't impress. As we were marched back towards the airport, more soldiers headed our way. White-naped pigeons flew overhead – but our bins remained untouched. We learned later that rebels were within 20 km of Addis Ababa and that the whole country was on high alert. Which might explain the sensitivity about two birders in 'combat gear' on the edge of an airport!

As I watch the Shoveler going round and round in ever decreasing circles, I wonder what life would be like if I had a normal job!

HORSEMEN RIDING BY

Wildlife artist and tour leader Eustace Barnes divides his time between his home in Kent and the jungles of South America. He recently illustrated a field guide to the birds of his favourite country, Peru.

Peru 1991. I was in Cusco, hoping to spot a piculet (a small woodpecker), thought to be a new species. There were only two other birders in Peru, so I set off on my quest with a Mancunian and a Swede. The local police allowed us up the valley, but made us sign a disclaimer that excused them of responsibility for our death or disappearance. They also kept our passports.

In the evening, we pitched camp at the degraded fragment of forest where the piculet had last been seen. As we fell asleep we heard a large group of horsemen trooping down the valley on the trail below.

Next morning, as dawn broke, we entered the cloud forest, but had a fruitless day searching for the piculet. We retired for beers and supper – and heard the horsemen pounding back up the valley.

After a restless night, we headed back to the village of Santa Teresa. All was pitch dark. Suddenly, as we arrived in the plaza, we were surrounded by armed boy soldiers. They appeared more terrified than we were,

and dismissed our explanation that we were watching birds. Tension continued to rise until the local police turned up with our passports. The soldiers vanished into the darkness.

The following morning, we learned that a group of mounted 'freedom fighters' had entered the village, rounded up a union leader and the local priest, conducted a mock trial and executed them in the plaza before disappearing back into the jungle.

Thankfully, Peru is a safe and welcoming country today, and I can travel it freely and without fear.

The Barn Owl: a beautiful, ghostly and ubiquitous species, and the most graceful hunter to watch at the time of day I most like hunting myself.

OUT FOR A DUCK

Richard Bashford was born in Sandy, so after leaving school it is hardly surprising that he went to work for the RSPB. In his spare time he scours the local gravel pits for birds and leads birdwatching tours. He is married to Katie and has a daughter, Molly.

Tour leading has its ups and downs. In one sense you're often working in wonderful places, seeing incredible wildlife spectacles and getting paid for it. On the other, you worry whether the birds will perform for your customers, and whether the experience will match the brochure!

One place I love to take tours is the Aqaba sewage works in Jordan. Here, I know my groups will never be disappointed. It is a real migration hotspot. The only problem is knowing which direction to look in first!

On one trip in April 1997, I was working through the wildfowl, when I spotted a small grey blob which awoke to reveal a short stubby goose-like bill. It was definitely a duck, but seemed smaller than the Teal, which is the smallest duck in Europe. The blob swam out onto the water, showing just how small it was. What on earth was it? Having at the time never been farther east into Asia, I dredged my memory, and tentatively thought it might be a Cotton Teal.

I consulted my copy of *The Birds of the Middle East*, which included vagrants to the Arabian peninsula, and this confirmed my hunch. What was more remarkable was that my sighting was the only western Palearctic record of this species, apart from the two I saw for sale in a market in Iraq in the 1970s. As if all this was not enough, it was also my birthday!

Later, I reflected that only a birder would be happy to spend his birthday in a sewage works in the Middle East.

The Hobby is a fantastic bird to watch, being a truly aerodynamic hunter with impressive fluid movements in the air.

THOSE EMBARRASSING MOMENTS

Bo Beolens is known as the 'Fat Birder'. His obsession with birds began when a Kingfisher landed on his fishing rod. Having taken time out for rock'n'roll and a family, he returned to the birding fold in his late thirties. He now runs the biggest birding website in the world. In 2000, Bo set up the Disabled Birders' Association to promote better access for disabled birders.

People often ask me what is my best birding moment or whether I have a favourite bird. The truth is I love every aspect of birding, from watching house sparrows from my study window to the spectacle of a million flamingos in Kenya's Rift Valley.

I have, however, often been embarrassed while birding. Once, when I was birding with my father on the Isle of Skye, a sudden downpour sent us scurrying into the car. As we waited for the rain to stop, we watched a black plastic bag fluttering in the wind, stuck to a bush high on a cliff. We shared our mutual disgust for such human detritus despoiling nature. Then the sun came out, and the black bag took to the air – miraculously transformed into a female Golden Eagle!

On another occasion in the Western Isles, my wife Maggie and I pulled into a lay-by to scan the hills. On

the ridge was a fine red deer stag. We were mesmerized too, by the clouds scudding over the purple heather, and transfixed by a superb male Hen Harrier that drifted over the ling and landed in the only stunted tree in sight. A cuckoo called hauntingly in the stillness.

We shared a sigh and a word or two about how wonderful it was to be out of sight of all things human…at which point, all around us camouflaged men festooned with heather and furze suddenly stood up, in unison, and an army radio squawked out a message of recall.

The Common Swift proves its reputation as one of the best fliers by feeding, sleeping and even mating on the wing.

STRANGER IN THE PARK

Keith Betton is the main spokesman for the UK travel industry, and a familiar face on TV (and voice on local and national radio). By his early 20s, he had been the youngest ever President of the London Natural History Society, and founded a highly-successful RSPB members' group.

As a lad, I lived in Hampton in south-west London, and was a regular visitor to Bushy Park. In June 1973, when I was 12 years old, I was exploring one of the plantations when I bumped into an old man. My Mum had told me not to talk to men in the park, and let's face it, how many 12-year-olds want to talk to anyone older than about 30, but ingrained politeness stopped me walking away, and we began to chat.

"Did you know that every Royal Park has an official bird observer?" he asked, after a few minutes.

I said that I did as I read their reports.

"Well, how would you like to be the official observer for Bushy Park?" he asked. Absolutely stunned, I said I'd love to. It turned out that I was talking to Lord Hurcomb, the Chairman of the Committee on Bird Sanctuaries in the Royal Parks.

"I'll appoint you to our committee", he promised and we arranged to meet again the following Sunday. On arriving home my mother and father were somewhat alarmed when I blurted out "Guess what? I've just met a man in the park...and he's a Lord!" Needless to say, my father insisted on accompanying me the next time we met. But Lord Hurcomb kept his word and a year later I went to the House of Lords to give my first report to the committee and then to Admiralty House to meet the Secretary of State for the Environment – an unusual experience for a 13-year-old! I later discovered that the official minimum age for observers was 18.

I spent every weekend for the next six years watching and recording birdlife in the Park, and established a lifetime passion.

The Tree Sparrow always attracted me because it lives in rural unspoilt areas and has a great personality.

25

KIDNAPPED!

Carl Buttle is a reformed, born-again non-twitcher who now concentrates on local birding in Suffolk and exotic foreign trips. His local patch at Benacre keeps him busy, with such goodies as Olivaceous Warbler, Bee-eater and Black Kite.

In April 2001, I was birding down a country lane in the Dominican Republic, looking for the giant Hispaniolan Lizard Cuckoo, when gradually I became aware of a youth following me. When I stopped, he stopped; when I started again, so did he.

Eventually I gave in and spoke to him. I spoke no Spanish, and he spoke very little English, but he did appear to be interested in the birds. After walking about 10 kilometres in sweltering heat, we came across a small village of dilapidated shanty huts, where we stopped to drink a welcome bottle of Coke.

The boy tried to persuade me that a bus would come along soon, but I didn't think that was very likely, so I began to walk. A few minutes later, however, a bus did come past and stopped a little ahead of me. I got on, to find myself the only passenger apart from the same boy, and another man who was drinking a bottle of beer.

But when we arrived at our destination – the town of Boca Chica – we had an argument about the bus fare. Suddenly they locked the doors and drove off – with me as prisoner! Fortunately, after a few minutes, the bus hit some traffic at the town's only roundabout. I took advantage of the momentary halt, squeezed out of the front window and dropped several metres to the ground.

I hate to think what terrible fate those three characters had been plotting for me. The good news is that I did manage to see the cuckoo – a brilliant bird!

Often hunting while it is still light, the Barn Owl's sheer beauty and agility cannot fail to impress as it quarters the meadows.

A REALLY GOOD TRIP

Clive Byers is an artist and illustrator. He has worked on a number of bird books, including The Handbook of the Birds of the World, A Guide to Buntings and Sparrows *and* Birds of the Indian Subcontinent. *When not painting, Clive works as a freelance bird tour leader and as a naturalist aboard cruise ships.*

It's 1979, a time when I was still young and impetuous. I'm with a group of fellow birders in northern Thailand. Driving all night and birding all day. We are heading for Nam Nao, following some 'gen'. We are given permission to take the road as long as we "go fast and don't stop for anything."

The day before, I had been given a rather large amount of marijuana. Not sure what to do with the stuff, I'd crammed it into a wooden pencil case (having removed the pencils, of course).

Then it's my turn to drive. We stop for a pee. I smoke a joint. I remember to drive fast without stopping. But I'm very stoned.

Great road, no traffic, Hot Punk pumping out of the stereo. I'm cruising…

Then suddenly, a roadblock! Serious uniforms. Guns. Waving. Shit! Think fast. Don't get busted. The stuff's on top of the dashboard. In a bloody pencil case!

Four other sleepy birders are dragged out of the car.

A Thai cop waves his gun. "Open the boot!" he orders.

The headline flashed in my mind: '25 Years for Drug-smuggling Birders'. We're waved into a line with our hands up, and body-searched armpits to crotch. I'm last in line, and desperately shuffle the pencil case into the back of the upper arm of my sweat shirt.

The cop doesn't find anything. He is perplexed, for he must have smelt it in the car. After a while he decides we can go. We get in the car and drive on. In the morning I got great views of the Rusty-naped Pitta. I've never seen it since.

The Common Swift, my favourite British bird, nests in my house and only comes to the UK in May, usually arriving on my birthday.

SINGLE-MINDED PURSUIT...

Richard Campey started birding under the influence of his school woodwork teacher, Kent birder Don Taylor. His serious birding began in the late 1970s when he lived on Lundy Island; after which he became a teacher himself. He is now a director of the optics firm In Focus.

What could be a more relaxing job than leading a cruise to Lundy Island to see some Puffins? My friend Keith Mortimer and I did just that and set off with our 250 eager customers.

We arrived at Lundy, spotted a few Puffins and started to point them out. Suddenly, a smaller bird flew into the cove, and plunged beneath the water. As it bobbed up on the surface the air turned as blue as the water, as Keith and I shouted simultaneously "what the **** was that?!"

It definitely wasn't a Puffin and we knew that we were looking at something exceptionally rare.

We now faced a dilemma. We were in charge of 250 paying customers whose sole aim was to see a Puffin, but all we wanted to do was identify the mystery bird. We spent a frustrating spell having to restrain our excitement as we pointed out Puffins to every member of our group.

Eventually another birder, John Waldon, joined us. Having been to Canada he was pretty sure it was either a murrelet or auklet. Keith and I abandoned our crowd and sprinted to the local tavern to fetch a copy of *Seabirds of the World*. We nailed the mystery bird as an Ancient Murrelet. It was the very first record for Britain and Europe, and the find of our lives.

With great pride and excitement, I announced this momentous news to the members of our group, but they were singularly unimpressed. As I left the boat, I overheard one couple saying that they'd had a lovely day but hadn't seen a Puffin, and that their guide had been preoccupied by some other strange bird. I pulled my coat hood over my face and sheepishly walked past!

As the nights turn dark and cold, I am lifted by the arrival of the Redwing with its fierce looks and eerie call.

TWENTY DEAF KANGAROOS

Tim Cleeves began birding at the age of 11 when he saw an advert for the Bristol Naturalists Society in a newsagent's window. He now works for the RSPB in Yorkshire. His wife Ann is an acclaimed writer of birding murder mysteries.

In spring 1975 we heard that a Subalpine Warbler had been trapped and ringed at Portland Bill in Dorset. So, one evening in April, three of us travelled from Bristol hoping to see the bird the following morning.

Right at the tip of Portland Bill, in front of the tall lighthouse, were some public toilets. Like most Gents toilets the ones at the Bill were fairly unsavoury so when we arrived at midnight, needing somewhere to sleep, we selected the drier and altogether pleasanter Ladies'. So about twenty birders from London and the West Country settled down into sleeping bags ready for a beer-fuelled sleep. But at around 1 am an ear-splitting sound reverberated inside the Ladies' toilet.

Since we'd gone to sleep, a sea mist had crept up over the Bill and the massive lighthouse foghorn had wailed into action. Swathed in our sleeping bags, we all hopped out of the toilet like deranged kangaroos, desperately trying to escape the tunnel of sound echoing around our bedroom. Having escaped the danger zone, we collapsed laughing.

A postscript to this event can be found in *Birding World* magazine. It seems that the rather pink-looking Subalpine Warbler we watched a few hours later was probably one of the geographical forms breeding in Corsica, Sardinia and the Balearic Islands not recorded in the UK before. So who knows, if this form is 'split' from the nominate cantillans one day, the near-deafening foghorn episode will have been well worth it.

I remember watching Red-backed Shrike in the New Forest. Twitching their tails, pouncing on insects and with wonderful colours – exquisite.

CELEBRITY VISITOR

Now retired, Peter Colston spent his working life as a museum curator, first at the Natural History Museum in London, and then in charge of one million bird specimens at Tring. Widely travelled, he has discovered and named several species new to science. He is also author of the best-selling Field Guide to the Rare Birds of Britain and Europe.

The Isles of Scilly have held a magnetic attraction for me ever since my first visit to St Agnes in 1958. My fourth trip, in 1964, coincided with a long spell of north-westerly winds and little of interest bird-wise.

The little island of Gugh lies just across from the larger island of St Agnes, connected at low tide by a sand bar, which it is possible to walk across. One blustery afternoon a lady living on Gugh noticed a pale object on the wall by the St Agnes quay opposite her house. Assuming it was her regular loaf of bread she wrapped herself up and set off across the sand bar with her small terrier.

Simultaneously, two young birders landed on the quay, wobbly-legged and pale-faced after a rough sea crossing. As they struggled to unload their gear the yapping of the lady's terrier caused them to look up. To their amazement, all they saw was a huge female Snowy Owl. It took off from the wall and flew across to Gugh – much to the surprise of the lady who imagined she had just seen her loaf of bread take wing!

Meanwhile, I was in the bird observatory when suddenly, the door burst open, and a wide-eyed and excited intruder stuttered: "There's a sn-sn-snow…".

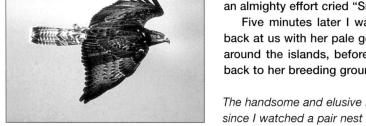

But his unfortunate stammer meant the words just wouldn't come out. I tried "Snow Bunting?" But he shook his head and with an almighty effort cried "Sn-snow-snowy Owl!!!"

Five minutes later I was watching this gorgeous bird staring back at us with her pale golden eyes. She spent the whole winter around the islands, before, I like to think, making the return trip back to her breeding grounds in the high Arctic.

The handsome and elusive Honey Buzzard has been a favourite since I watched a pair nest in the New Forest in the 1950s.

MISTAKEN IDENTITY

Dominic Couzens has a regular column in Bird Watching *magazine, is the author of several books, and wrote and co-produced the* Teach Yourself Bird Sounds *cassettes. He also leads adult education classes and birding tours, mainly in Britain, but has also been to Spain, Portugal, Bulgaria, Canada, Madagascar, Trinidad and Jordan. He lives in Dorset with his wife and daughter.*

A friend of mine was due to lead a bird club outing. But at the last minute he had to pull out and he asked me to fill in for him. So, a few days later I found myself in a coach full of strangers arriving at Abberton Reservoir in Essex.

The 30 or so birdwatchers set off for the visitor centre while I finalized rendezvous details with the driver. This took longer than expected, so I was slightly anxious that the group would be hanging around getting cold and impatient. Sure enough, there was a knot of people hanging around outside the centre, watching the birds at the feeders. I mumbled an apology and got on with the job I was there to do.

I firmly believe in describing interesting aspects of bird behaviour as well as giving tips on identification. There were several Dunnocks by one of the feeders, which presented the perfect opportunity for a good story. I immediately regaled the assembled throng with all the fascinating details of the species' notorious sexual appetite. Multiple partners, sex in the bushes, rejection of sperm...I warmed to the subject and packed in every lurid detail. After all, I wanted to prove my worth as an informed and interesting leader. I did wonder about the sidelong glances but ignored them.

Then I noticed someone waving at me from another group of people further down the track. Several of them started waving. Realization dawned. My birding group was already halfway to the first hide. So, whoever I had been talking to, it wasn't them.

I never tire of seeing the clean, crisp and immaculate Firecrest; it isn't rare, but you have to work for it as it never gives itself up easily.

EVERY BIRD LOVES A DOCTOR

Based in Essex, Simon Cox combined his professional life as a GP and Police Surgeon with his hobby as a birder for 34 years, before retiring in 2002. He has published many articles on birds, as well as editing A New Guide to the Birds of Essex.

Though I was a full-time GP and Police Surgeon for more than a third of a century, my wife Pat once described me as an ornithologist who dabbles in medicine in his spare time! Certainly, combining a busy medical career with an obsessive interest in birds has had its moments.

Two Sundays on call come to mind. On one, an elderly lady asked in a querulous voice, "Are you the bird doctor?" On being told yes, she continued, "Would you come and cut my budgie's toenails?"

On another, Sunday lunch was interrupted by the arrival of a police officer carrying a cardboard box. I took it indoors, and opened the lid, at which point a sprightly Ruff leapt out and landed on the dining table in front of my speechless father-in-law, narrowly missing the roast beef!

Then there was the patient who asked to use our 'facilities'. I had forgotten about the Great Black-backed Gull that was recuperating in the shower tray and which duly emerged to inspect the patient at a crucial moment! Pat also recalls driving into our garage one winter's night to find a strange object suspended from a beam. It was a dead Gadwall, left for me by a patient, because it was wearing a ring.

My star patient? Undoubtedly the well-informed bank manager who phoned me about an unusual bird seen near the marina where he kept his boat. It proved to be a splendid male Citrine Wagtail – the first adult of this species ever recorded in the British Isles. Who said that life in the NHS is dull!

Essentially black and white in breeding dress, the Black-throated Diver has a subtle elegance as it glides through the water.

BRIEF ENCOUNTER

After completing his Master's degree in the Ecuadorian Cloud Forest, Mike Dilger spent over five years working in the forests of Vietnam, Tanzania, Peru and Costa Rica. He wrote and presented two natural history specials and a six-part series for Channel 5. He now works at the BBC Natural History Unit.

I was in Ecuador, hoping particularly to see the rare and enigmatic Long-wattled Umbrella-bird. This crow-sized bird has a wonderful black crest that it flicks up at will. The male's wattle hangs from its chest like the frill of an Adam Ant shirt and is inflated to attract females. I was guiding a group of birders around a reserve, and after a couple of days, we had logged about 150 species, but the Long-wattled Umbrella-bird had eluded us. On the last morning, we rose at dawn for one last foray into the jungle.

I was at the front, when someone at the back spotted a Broad-billed Motmot. Everyone else went back to have a look, but my birder's sixth sense told me to take a look round the upcoming corner. There, slap-bang in front of me was the Long-wattled Umbrella-bird.

My mouth went dry, my legs went wobbly, and I lifted my bins. The bird looked at me, raised its crest and momentarily inflated its wattle...I was in heaven!

I had to get the group back to see this, but in my excitement, instead of quietly retreating, I momentarily lost my finely honed birding skills and yelled at the top of my voice:

"Come quick!"

Not surprisingly, the bird disappeared like smoke into the trees just as the group came charging around the corner.

"What, what?" they shouted in unison.

"Long-wattled Umbrella-bird," I croaked.

There was a moment's silence, then one of the group uttered the immortal phrase: "Why did you shout then, you stupid prick?"

The Roseate Tern never looks so fine as when it first arrives from its West African winter quarters, resplendent in its breeding plumage.

TWO STUPID ALIENS

Dave Farrow lives in Norwich, and has been travelling the globe in search of birds for over 20 years. He currently leads tours for Birdquest, focusing mainly on Asia and the Middle East.

"I am from the Public Security Organ! You are in an area of national security and defence! You have broken the law governing the movement of aliens within the Peoples' Republic of China! You are under arrest!"

The Chinese policeman stood menacingly in the doorway of our crude Tibetan doss house. Fellow birder Craig Robson and I had survived a gruelling five-day trek over high mountain passes and through snowstorms, living on little other than biscuits, fags and scenery. We had just rediscovered Kozlov's Bunting which had not been seen since the 1930s. And now we were busted. At that time, in 1986, many parts of Tibet were still out of bounds to foreigners.

"You must pay fine!" the policeman ordered, but then reconsidered.

"No, as you are first foreigner since Revolution, you must write self-criticism instead."

And so we did: 'I am very sorry, I am very stupid, I am sorry that I have broken the law governing the movement of aliens within the Peoples' Republic of China, I love China and the Chinese people...' We were then put on the bus to the next open city, Xining, 800 kilometres away. Our passports were sent on, and we had to collect them from the Office of the Public Security Bureau...who obviously had the same rule book:

"You have broken the law," they announced. "You must pay fine! But you are first foreigner since Revolution, so instead you must write self-criticism."

"Righto then, here you go," we replied cheerfully, "er, and where can we get a visa extension?"

"Oh – just over there, in the next office!"

My favourite bird is the Jack Snipe because it is cryptic and skulking, just as real birds should be – and a challenge to find.

SOMEONE TO WATCH OVER ME

Born and raised in Derbyshire's Peak District, Brian Gee, along with his partner Fay Enright, gave up work in 1992 to travel the world for over two years in search of birds. Brian still eschews the rat-race, financing his global trips with various types of freelance work.

During the Indonesian sector of our World birding trip, Fay and I came across some scruffy, hand-written notes in the possession of another birder with instructions on where to find what was tantalizingly described as 'the best bird in the world' – Wilson's Bird-of-Paradise.

The thrill of embarking on a treasure hunt mixed with the trepidation of setting off into the unknown as we duly boarded a ferry to Irian Jaya. After two days of negotiations we organized the charter of a motorized canoe setting off to Batanta one of only two small islands where 'Wilson's BoP' – as it is known – is found. At our destination we arranged a guide, Ayoub, from the tiny Papuan stilted settlement.

That night we slept deeply, waking at dawn to find large land crabs squabbling over the remains of our bananas. Wilson's BoP only displays in the early morning, so our guide led us through the forest at lightning pace, cutting a path with his sharp parang. A speedy climb gave us pounding hearts and thumping heads, as we were running on a mix of adrenaline and caffeine – as the crabs had deprived us of anything more.

The male Wilson's BoP will not tolerate any green vegetation in his display ground, so when we arrived

at an area stripped of foliage, Ayoub applied his master stroke. He cut a stick, lashed ferns to the top, then planted it in the middle of the display ground. Within minutes, a technicolor apparition had alighted on the mock fern and started to destroy it. He did not rest until every piece of offending greenery was safely removed. As we crouched transfixed by the performance and the sheer gaudiness of this bizarre bird, we noticed that Ayoub was sitting there with a huge grin, watching us watching 'the best bird in the world'.

For me, the charismatic Dipper epitomizes the rugged Peak District with its sublime adaptation to a harsh environment.

WHERE THE SUN DON'T SHINE...

Neil Glenn lives in Nottingham, about as far from the coast (where many rare birds turn up) as you can get in Britain. He works as a laboratory assistant at the University, but this doesn't stop him dashing off to see rare birds at the drop of a hat. Neil recently wrote Best Birdwatching Sites in Norfolk *and is an avid football fan, supporting Notts County. His best days out are those that combine a twitch with a pitch.*

This birding tale of woe demonstrates what we mad birders have to endure to earn the title of 'twitcher'!

A few Septembers ago, a friend and I agreed that if a really rare bird turned up anywhere in the country, we would book a day off work and go for it, no matter where it was. So when my pager informed me, at 11 pm one Tuesday, that a Baltimore Oriole had turned up on the Isles of Scilly, we just had to go. My wife's reaction to the news is not fit to print.

By six the next morning we were at Penzance heliport, where we learned to our dismay that all the helicopters were full. There was no alternative but to dash across to St Just to catch the plane. As the daily boat from St Mary's to Bryher (where the bird had been seen the day before) was due to leave just as we were landing, the pilot radioed ahead. We caught the boat. Next problem: a very rough crossing. Thankfully, the boat didn't sink, but our mood did. We spent the whole day wandering the lanes with only a few thrushes and blackbirds for company. It was obvious the bird had flown.

We were trudging downheartedly back towards the quay, when an islander approached us.

"I had a lovely bird on my bird table yesterday – beautiful orangey thing, some sort of American oriole apparently," he said.

Which reminds me, I must retrieve my tripod from 'where the sun don't shine' the next time I am on Bryher.

Neil has had better luck with the Firecrest, his favourite British bird: a little gem with subtle shades of olive-greens and orange.

DREAM BIRD

Mark Golley was one of the youngest birders in the UK to reach the magic 400 species (at the tender age of 20). But it's not just twitching that excites, he'd rather watch a Neil Young gig any day.

It's July 1989. I'm the Shorebird Protection Warden at Gibraltar Point NNR. A busy weekend has just cost me my dream bird, the Blue-cheeked Bee-eater. Then, just days later, comes a second bite at the cherry.

The agony of missing the bee-eater at Cowden was beginning to ease: black humour mixed with copious amounts of liquid sedation had quelled the pain. It was a lovely day at Gibraltar Point. Then the phone rang.

Someone from the eerie flatlands was calling to say he was sure there was a Blue-cheeked Bee-eater outside his house. Frantically, cover was sorted and eventually it was "LET'S GO!"

And go we did, like the wind, to Destination: bee-eater! As we approached, panic set in. Where were we? Was it left, right or straight on? In the heat-hazed distance an unmistakable silhouette hawked from telephone wires. But we were lost. A crop sprayer did a treetop flyover. "Bloody show-off", we muttered.

A wrong turn here, a dead end there, but eventually a smiling face greeted us. 'It must still be here.' I thought. 'He's smiling. We saw it as an unmistakable speck 20 minutes ago. And he *is* smiling…'

"It was here half an hour ago", came the beaming opening salvo. The rest was a blur. I heard "crop sprayer" and "made it fly away" but the salty tears were already pricking my eyes. The same bird, an incredible second chance, stolen from us by the Treetop Flyer.

As the summer faded, there was an Open Day at the reserve.

"Hello" beamed a strangely familiar face. "I've got a photo of that Blue-cheeked Bee-eater. Would you like to see it?" A small part of me collapsed again. A pin-prick-sized green image was never so hurtful. And to this day, some fourteen years on, the pain remains and that little square on my UK list is still empty.

For me, Firecrest is the near-perfect bird. A tiny, agile, paint box bundle…and it's far easier to see than a Blue-cheeked Bee-eater!

49

TWO TICKS AND A CROSS

Chris Harbard cut his birding teeth at Spurn Head and became a serious twitcher during the 1970s. After joining the RSPB in 1979, he became one of Britain's best-known publicists for birding, via radio and TV interviews. He has also written two pub quiz books on birds.

One fateful day in May, a bunch of RSPB colleagues and I dashed off to Norfolk, in search of the Desert Warbler and the Oriental Pratincole.

We drove straight to Cley and tramped along the shingle to where the warbler was performing perfectly. What a great bird, posing, singing, even gathering nest material! WOW!

Then, after a quick bite to eat in the Coastguards' café, on to the village of Gimingham to search for the pratincole. It took us a while, but eventually we saw it. Two great British ticks before lunch! As we returned to the car park, I thought it was odd that ours was the only car there. Absolutely everyone else had gone!

When I got home, my wife greeted me:

"Well did you see it?"

"Saw both of them." I said, feeling rather smug.

"Oh, were there two? Duncan only mentioned one" she said. I was puzzled, "Duncan...??"

"Yes, he rang to say did you want to go up to Norfolk for the swift and I said you were already there and must be watching it..." she said. I was still confused. "Swift???"

"Yes, the Pacific Swift, or something...he said it was very rare."

I didn't feel like lunch. And I didn't stop swearing for three days. Why didn't we realize why everyone had suddenly left? Why didn't we notice everyone's pagers going off? Why didn't we check by phone before going home?

However hard I try to remember the pleasure of seeing the warbler and the pratincole on that sunny May day, I can't.

The Great Grey Shrike was the first, and perhaps the most exciting, 'rare' bird I have ever found – behind my house in Yorkshire in 1967.

51

NOT WAVING BUT DROWNING...

Andy Jarrett is a freelance sculptor, based in Norwich. When not exhibiting and trying to sell his work, he teaches environmental education for a project working with schools. His local patch is the Yare Valley.

The Yare Valley was at its very best on this particular Saturday afternoon, as I set out in my recently acquired kayak canoe for a spot of birding.

A blast from a Cetti's Warbler came from the reeds; Black-headed Gulls wheeled, and a Marsh Harrier glided overhead. As I paddled towards the River Yare I noticed an elderly couple walking along the bank.

Suddenly, I dug my paddle too deeply into the water and instantly capsized. I was totally shocked. My scope was in the canoe, and at first this was my main concern. But, as I splashed around with the canoe still on top of me, I realized my feet were trapped. My whole body was under water, and no amount of kicking would set me free. Meanwhile, my arms whirled wildly in the water. The world around me was black and cold. An immense, swirling pain filled my head. I knew I couldn't last much longer.

As my energy ran out, a final burst of frenzied kicking miraculously worked. The darkness cracked with an explosion of light as I surfaced and gasped for air. As my face turned to the air I remember seeing my drawing pencils floating around me.

Later, bedraggled and wet, I met the couple I had seen earlier. The woman, greeted me with a smile.

"Hello. We saw you out there waving to us. We did wave back!" Amazingly, they thought my thrashing arms was a cheerful hello.

I still regularly undertake 'pollution-free birding' from a canoe, and have managed to twitch Great White Egret, Whiskered Tern, Baird's Sandpiper, Lesser Yellowlegs and White-winged Black Tern. I am of course now much more careful to stay on the surface!

I used to see good numbers of Hen Harriers, even as a garden bird, wintering in the Yare Valley in the late nineties. I rarely see any now.

BIRD NUT

Chris Kightley runs Limosa Holidays, a successful bird tour company, from his home in Norfolk. He is a frequent contributor to Birdwatching Magazine *and developed and co-wrote the acclaimed* Pocket Guide to the Birds of Britain and Northwest Europe. *Chris is married to his business partner Barbara.*

It was the first day of our Wild Goose Chase, a tour of Holland we do every winter. As we met at the airport, our guide Arnoud told us of a change of plan: instead of heading off to watch geese, we were diverting to Rotterdam to look for a Nutcracker – a rare member of the crow family.

We drove up and down for some time, and kept finding ourselves in dead-end roads. Finally we stumbled across the right place: a parking lot surrounded by trees, with a couple of local bird photographers hanging about.

One old boy was throwing monkey nuts to the Nutcracker, which flew down to grab one, then headed off into the trees to bury it, before coming back again. I was watching, when I felt a tap on my shoulder, and turned round to find this old boy pointing at my head! I eventually realized that he was suggesting that I put a nut on my head to see what happened. So I did, and stood and waited by the trees, feeling a bit of a nutter, but wondering if the bird would indeed take the bait.

Lo and behold, it did! I heard a whirr of wings, felt a clunk, actually more a surprisingly heavy thud, and Arnoud pressed the shutter button of his camera.

It was super way to start the holiday, really memorable! The only trouble is I've never been allowed to forget it, and every time I lead a trip the group speculates about which bird will land on my head this time!

The Long-tailed Tit's cheerful and distinctive call is often the first sign of life on a winter's walk; always eliciting a sense of excitement.

FANCY A SHAG?

Justin Lansdell is a 30-year-old Norfolk birder, for whom balancing wildfowl counts in his beloved Yare Valley with a responsible job as an IT manager is a way of life. He has been known to hire helicopters for a long-distance twitch.

For 18 years (yes, I was pounding a local patch aged 12!) birding has allowed me to indulge in all my passions: travelling to far-flung places, meeting similarly obsessed folk, and satisfying the need to occasionally do something spontaneous and totally off-the-wall.

Those familiar with Norfolk's impressive avifauna will know that for all our galaxy of riches, we don't get Shags often enough. Therefore, the discovery a few years ago of a number of these seabirds wintering at Lowestoft in the neighbouring county of Suffolk was an exciting event.

After a whole series of nocturnal visits to the roost site, numbers reached an impressive ten birds, but temperatures on the exposed south pier, from which they were visible, often plummeted below freezing. It was a particularly cold December night in Norwich when I was nightclubbing with my girlfriend and my pager bleeped through the message "Suffolk: 11 Shags under floodlights in Lowestoft Harbour this evening".

Instantly, the image of the binoculars in my glovebox flashed into my mind. I was in the car within minutes, my girlfriend summarily abandoned, left completely dumbstruck on the dancefloor.

I did return to the deserted nightclub a couple of hours later, warmed (despite wearing only a thin shirt) by the memory of the peak Shag count, to find my girlfriend sitting inside with only the cleaners for company. We are no longer together.

Have I mended my ways with girls? No. But my current long-term girlfriend has visited Lowestoft Harbour after dark, and there are now two pairs of binoculars in the glovebox of my car.

When I saw my first Snowy Owl it was so perishingly cold that I cried (I always claimed this was due to elation – until now!).

SPANISH INQUISITION

After winning the British Birds Bird Illustrator of the Year competition in 1985, Ian Lewington embarked on a highly successful career as a bird artist. He is a member of the British Ornothological Union Records Committee and lives in Oxfordshire where he is involved in many bird population monitoring projects.

In common with other bird illustrators, I have a disturbing fascination for dead birds – purely, of course, so that I can examine the subtleties of their plumage in close-up. In 1991, my wife Debbie and I were travelling through southern Spain when we came across a couple of Corn Buntings that had been killed on the road. I put them in the car boot for later examination.

We spent the day searching for the elusive White-rumped Swift in the mountains. After fleeting views, we headed up the mountain on a pot-holed minor road, which bizarrely then turned into a smooth tarmac highway. Curiously, it was not marked on our map. We soon found out why. We drove round a bend to come face-to-face with a large military installation. We swiftly turned around, but unfortunately were caught up by two military police on motorbikes. None of us could speak the others' language, but using sign language they made it clear they wanted to search the car.

They soon found the Corn Buntings, and their friendly tone changed to one of suspicion. They obviously thought we had illegally shot the birds. Debbie furiously flicked through the phrasebook for suitable words, while I showed them my sketchbook. No dice. Finally, Debbie came up with the key words 'artist', and 'road kill'. The soldiers exchanged a few disbelieving words, and after a pregnant pause uttered a simple command: "Okay – Go!"

I have never been so glad to be back on a bum-numbing road!

The dazzling injection of colour that Yellow Wagtails bring to early spring really excites me, particularly when flocks of migrants arrive.

GOODNESS GRACIOUS ME!

Tony Marr started birding as a Sussex schoolboy, over 50 years ago, and has the notebooks to prove it! Today, he lives in north Norfolk but leads birding tours all over the world. He has a particular interest in sea birds and works as an ornithologist and lecturer on expedition cruise ships in the Arctic and Antarctic.

In early 1979, I went on a birding trip with Bill Oddie and some other friends. At the time, The Goodies was attracting millions of TV viewers every week, and Bill was at the height of his fame in his original incarnation as a comedy actor. I wasn't surprised that while we were waiting at Heathrow Airport, lots of people came up and asked for autographs, though I was a bit taken aback when some guy started filming Bill as he was sleeping on the plane!

In many ways, Bill is a shy, private man, who finds being in the limelight uncomfortable. So at first I think he was relieved that in India he could walk around like any British visitor, unknown to the locals.

Then, one day, we decided to visit the Taj Mahal. We were standing in the queue waiting to buy our entry tickets when an Indian-looking gentleman came up to Bill, and without any hesitation announced:

"You are Bill Oddie of The Goodies!"

We were astonished that our friend was instantly recognized, and I asked Bill if the programme was on Indian TV. He said he didn't think so. So I turned to the Indian and asked him how he recognized Bill.

"Because I'm a Goodies fan on holiday from Bradford."

A little later, we were standing on the balcony of the Taj, looking across the heavily polluted river, when a human corpse floated by with a vulture perched on it. "Hey Bill, what do you make of that?" I asked. "Looks like a White-backed to me..." came his reply.

The Barn Owl is the most graceful bird imaginable. With its white plumage and silent flight, it has a ghostly appearance as it hunts.

KINDRED SPIRIT

Brought up in the west London suburbs, Neil McKillop led a solitary early birding life, apart from the odd coach trip with the local Young Ornithologists' Club group.

In the early 70s, sex, drugs and rock'n'roll were among the many distractions to take my mind off birding. And as old passport photos bear witness, I was a fully paid-up weekend hippie. It just wouldn't have been, well, cool, to mention to anyone that I enjoyed watching birds!

Then this bloke began to frequent the record shop where I 'worked'. He was called Phil Hurrell, and looked even more bohemian than me. We listened to records, drank tea, listened to more records and drank even more tea.

One day, I put on a record by Roy Harper called Stormcock, which featured a photo of a Mistle Thrush nest on the back cover, together with a sleeve note reference to *The Observer's Book of Birds*. One track featured lines such as 'but the robin outside has to hunt and hide in the cold and frosty shire', and 'the cuckoo she moves through the dawn fanfare'.

I happened to draw Phil's attention to these odd references to birds and mentioned another song by Pink Floyd which featured a recording of a Blackcap's song.

Phil looked at me curiously, and quietly mumbled: "Are you interested in birds, then?"

I realized I had found a fellow enthusiast – albeit a closet one. I admitted my passion and the two of us travelled the length and breadth of Britain in search of birds, until Phil decided he needed something more exotic and headed off on a world birding tour.

I've never managed to get my daughters interested in birding, although my girlfriend has accompanied me occasionally – well, you've got to have someone to carry your scope, haven't you!

Birds of prey are favourites of mine and the seemingly effortless and elegant agility of the Hobby never fails to impress.

MEN BEHAVING BADLY

Derek Moore has an OBE for services to conservation and has been a birder 'from the womb'. He has travelled around the world and is now the Chief Executive of the Wildlife Trust for South and West Wales.

It was May 1987 and my first real birding trip to Spain. We were the most unlikely group of four with nothing in common except a fanatical passion for birdwatching. There was Malcolm, an English Nature warden who caught the first spring Dusky Warbler in the UK. Mike was a nurseryman who had the audacity to move into my native Suffolk from birdless Oxford and turn out to be rather good. Melvyn was a newcomer to the birding scene and a high-flying Volvo salesman who provided us with the most expensive and latest model for this trip over the Pyrenees and into the Ebro Delta in Spain.

We had a tent. One member of the team disgusted the hard men of the party by bringing a camp bed, brushed cotton pyjamas and insisting on a full English breakfast every morning. He in turn, sneered at the rest of us who just kicked our boots off, slept, woke and were out birding before he stirred. But nobody told us how cold it was going to be at night in the mountains, and so in the end, we all abandoned the tent and sought solace in local hotels.

In our enthusiasm, we made some mistakes: a cow pat was identified as a Pine Marten and a light aircraft as a Lammergeier. But there were also moments of pure joy: real Lammergeiers over snowy tops, glorious Rock Thrushes on the scree, tiny Citril Finches in the stunted trees, and we added such gems as Pin-tailed and Black-bellied Sandgrouse and Dupont's Lark to our lists. We scoffed at Mike when he said he'd spotted Herring Gulls with red bills, but then we all caught sight of these hordes of Audouin's Gulls. They were not expected at all and became the worst kept secret in that part of Spain for years.

My favourite British bird is the goggle-eyed Stone Curlew with its startling golden eye and piercing call.

65

ONE GOOD DEED DESERVES ANOTHER

Neil Morris began twitching in the late 70s. After studying Botany and Zoology at Bristol, he worked at the RSPB, where he worked for six years. He has pursued a career in marketing for non-profit organizations and is currently Deputy Managing Director of The Institute of Direct Marketing, an educational trust.

Let me start by saying that I am no religious zealot or even a 'believer'. But one cold, grey day in October 1993, I truly considered the existence of God.

Mike Langman and I had scoured every bush and field on a blustery Dorset headland but found nothing. Hungry, cold and wet, I was lagging behind when a car came down the track and stopped at a closed gate. A small, fragile-looking, silver–haired elderly lady attempted to clamber out, but I gave in to my better nature, retraced my steps, and opened the gate for her, and guided car and driver through. I vividly remember thinking, "If there is a God, that good deed deserves something in return."

And that's when it happened: a subliminal flash of blue on a passing Robin. It was the briefest glimpse out of the corner of my eye; nothing certain at all. Yet something compelled me to stay rooted to that spot. And, after what seemed like an age, up it popped again. It was like manna from heaven. Twenty years of poring over bird books and fantasizing about finding 'the big one', had finally brought me the Red–flanked Bluetail. The rest, as they say, is twitching history and, ever since, my birdwatching has taken twice as long as I'm forever stopping to perform good deeds – to help another senior citizen or pick up litter – I once even broke off mid–twitch to join the search for a missing guide dog!

Call me cynical, but I feel I need one more piece of proof. So if you're listening, God, haven't I done enough now to earn a Siberian Rubythroat? Next October, in Dorset again, would be a fine time for my final conversion to the faith!

Most definitely Neil's favourite British bird, the Winspit Red–flanked Bluetail gave him a place in twitching history.

NO TURKISH DELIGHT

One of Britain's leading bird artists, Dave Nurney was born in London and then moved to Surrey when he was 13 years old. By the time he went to art college, his first drawings had been published by the local newspaper. After joining a Bird Club in 1977, he travelled extensively and built his knowledge and love of birds. He is married and has a son.

We were young, we were birders, and we were in Turkey. We slept in the car – or under it – and ate bread rolls, jam and oranges. One day, we drove for 14 hours with only a break for Masked Shrike. We'd seen most of Turkey's lowland specialities and now we were aiming for the mountains, hoping to get to the Black Sea and hopefully see Wallcreeper.

We came to a small alpine road that wound through a gorge (no Wallcreeper). As the hired Fiat estate emerged into the sunshine, we came face-to-face with a giant brown slug. At least that's what the mudslide looked like. It was 2 metres high and blocked the road.

"Drive over it", suggested Shaun helpfully from the back. But even I wouldn't put a hire car through this, so regretfully we turned back, scouring the high cliffs of the gorge (no Wallcreeper).

We tried another pass. After 40 kilometres it came to a dead-end. It began to rain. Seriously. On our return route, a puddle on a bend turned into a quagmire, with a 30-metre drop to one side. The lads got out, and tried to plug the sea of mud with rocks, wood, dead goats, etc.

I revved up the engine, shot forward, there was a meaty clang, and lots of bouncing. I heaved on the handbrake, the Fiat's back end shot round and I careered towards the precipice, but missed it, sending wood and dead goats flying.

Four muddy birders climbed back into the car, and we headed down the mountain. (No Wallcreeper).

Firecrest is my favourite because it has everything – character, eyestripes, wing bars and if you find one, it's always a good day.

MAIDEN FLIGHT

Martin Palmer's childhood interest in garden birds took serious hold following his marriage and move to Bedfordshire in November 1971. Martin has kept detailed daily records of his sightings ever since, and has around 480 species on his British list, half of them in Bedfordshire.

It is 24 October, 1981. I am keenly anticipating my second trip to the Isles of Scilly. On my first I had been very seasick, so this time I decided to fly. Orphean Warbler awaited and so nine birders had chartered a plane from St Just, Cornwall (there was no Skybus then).

The decrepit flying club seemed deserted on our arrival: unwashed glasses littered the bar and springs protruded from the sofa. We were surprised by the sudden entry of an immaculately uniformed pilot. But we had to push the aged twin-engine plane out of the hangar. Mentally, I checked for metal fatigue.

Individual doors along the rectangular fuselage gave entry to pairs of seats. Scopes and luggage were stowed, then birders two by two. This was my first ever flight and I hung back nervously. "You're up here

with me" beckoned our pilot. Old car seat belts and British Rail ashtrays were affixed to the doors. A steering wheel and array of dials were before me in my co-pilot's seat. Having no watch himself, the pilot used mine to coordinate with the control tower. After take-off, relieved but still nervous, I offered the skipper a cigarette, and he accepted.

A short while later, he announced "fags out, we're coming in to land!"

He tried to stub out his cigarette, but the ash-tray crashed to floor. "Quick, take the controls!" he yelled, bending to find the smouldering butt. I gripped the wheel, and glanced over my shoulder at my grimacing companions. My first ever flight, and I was flying the bloody plane!

Nevertheless, the pilot made a very smooth landing to spontaneous applause...we travelled back by boat!

Who can deny the thrill of hearing the enigmatic Herring Gull's raucous calls from a seaside rooftop. A definite favourite with me.

SUN, SEA, SAND...AND NUNS

Tony Smith began birding at the age of seven, and persuaded his father to give him binoculars for passing the 11-plus. Since then he has birded in over 70 countries and seen well over half the world's bird species. After a career in the Civil Service, he now lives and birds in Norfolk.

The Mauritius police were first alerted to our presence when they moved us on from the quiet parking spot we had found near the airport soon after our arrival. Apparently it was the site of a busy street market.

After a night in the police station, we had a visit from the local police chief. With him was the only birding copper on the island who had been given the day off so he could take us to the best birding sites on Mauritius. In no time he had found the Mauritius Kestrel and Pink Pigeon, two of the rarest birds in the world.

To celebrate with a few beers, we headed for a local bar. It was a bit dark, and considering that we were the only customers, it seemed rather overstaffed with scantily-clad barmaids. Soon the penny dropped as we realized that beer was far from being the prime commodity on sale.

So, we moved on to an idyllic spot from which we could sea-watch. Then, a dishevelled figure approached, sold us a soapstone carving of a Dodo, and warned us that a massive cyclone was on its way.

We decided to head back towards the airport, but the cyclone hit *en route*. Trees were torn from the ground, debris flew through the air and it rained coconuts. We headed for shelter in what looked like a church. But the door was opened by a nun – it was a convent!

The next day, as I packed to leave, I came across a pile of magazines depicting male body-builders. I've no idea what they were they doing in a convent. Another of life's unsolved mysteries.

We thanked the nuns for their hospitality and emerged to a scene of utter devastation. We eventually got home via Singapore.

24 December, 1970, I find a Ross's Gull at South Shields, and so Christmas is cancelled as birders flock to see this mythical species.

LOVE IN A COLD CLIMATE

David Tipling is one of Britain's leading bird photographers. In 1998, after reading Apsley Cherry-Garrard's The Worst Journey in the World, *he became obsessed with reaching an Emperor Penguin rookery and documenting life in the colony on film.*

It is said that a man cannot look at a penguin without smiling. This was certainly the case with me when I saw my first penguins – a magnificent colony of Emperors. These enigmatic birds proved to be delightfully co-operative, and they were set among some of the world's most spectacular scenery.

We were camping at temperatures of minus 30°C – which presents some interesting challenges. How do you keep your toothpaste from freezing, for example? I tried washing my hair, but it promptly froze solid. At night you pee into a bottle – which must then be kept in your sleeping bag so that it doesn't freeze and can be emptied in the morning. Washing was such an act of courage, that we didn't, at all.

For six days, I was in photographic heaven taking amazing shots of my wonderfully enigmatic subject. On the seventh day, we ran out of toilet paper and used snow instead, our rations were reduced to bacon and maple syrup, and a storm hit. The storm raged for three days. We managed to reach the colony on two days but once we were nearly lost in a whiteout. It was worth the effort, though. We found huge crèches of young huddled together in the driving snow, and although it was almost impossible to operate a camera in the conditions, I managed to take some memorable images.

On the tenth day, we heard bangs and creaking: the sea ice on which we were camping was breaking up. Time to move on! The flight home was hair-raising. We almost ran out of fuel twice: the first time we had to make a forced landing on sea ice; the second time we were so low on fuel that we had to taxi across the ice to the fuel dump. Finally, though, we reached the base camp at Patriot Hills, and were welcomed with very cold Champagne.

Only the size of a sparrow, the Storm Petrel has a remarkable lifestyle, living most of its life offshore, flitting just above the waves.

ALL STEAMED UP

Ray Turley began serious birding in the early 1960s at Romford sewage farm, though nowadays he does most of his birding at Dungeness. He was a pioneering twitcher when the hobby took root in the 70s, and makes beautiful sculptures of birds in his spare time.

At 5 o'clock one May morning, I woke to the sound of a strong north-westerly wind and rain. I went back to sleep. I'd been up at dawn every morning for two months to seawatch at Dungeness, so I felt I deserved a lie-in. But at 7.20, the phone rang – which at that time of the morning could only mean one thing. A rare bird.

It was Mike Buckland. In a hurried but precise voice, he announced: "This is not a joke. There is a Black-browed Albatross, sat on the sea about half a mile out from the seawatching hide at Dungeness".

My reply was short and to the point: "It had better not be a joke – see you soon". Pulling up my trousers, tying my shoelaces, I legged it outside, grabbing my optics, coat and gloves as I went.

The previous day, I'd replaced a punctured tyre on my car with an emergency tyre that wasn't supposed to be driven over 40 mph. I have now discovered they can go much faster without exploding! I set a new speed record between Greatstone and Dungeness; followed by another for sprinting while carring a tripod down to the seawatch hide. This was a bad move, as I was by now very hot and my optics were very cold, so they kept steaming up. Other observers offered their scopes but I had the same problem. The bird was there but I couldn't see it! I had to calm down; and stay calm.

After several attempts to de-fog my scope, I was able to see the albatross for the first time, but it had drifted well out to sea. It was not the best view in the world, but I could see it was an albatross. Then I noticed another birdwatcher sitting on the beach, so I raced to tell him the news. To my amazement, he seemed completely unimpressed. I returned to the hide, just in time to see the albatross glide effortlessly over the horizon. I wonder if that bloke ever realized what he'd missed!

The elusive Wallcreeper favours inaccessible cliffs, which makes it all the more rewarding when you catch its crimson flash as it flicks its wings.

WAR REPORT

Brian Unwin, a lifelong birder, played a leading part in founding the Durham Bird Club and Whitburn Observatory. He spent 13 years with the Press Association, but now works as a freelance wildlife writer from his South Tyneside home.

The ice patrol ship HMS Endurance was on what should have been its final South Atlantic adventure when I was given permission to spend three weeks on board as a journalist.

I joined the ship at Montevideo, Uruguay, and we sailed on New Year's Eve 1981. The next day, as we pitched violently in a storm, Wandering and Black-browed Albatrosses escorted us. We also saw Great Shearwaters and Atlantic Petrels. The seabird list grew impressively as we pushed further south.

Almost a week later we were off the Antarctic Peninsula, Adélie Penguins watched us from ice floes and all-white Snow Petrels, with delicate, bat-like flight ghosted alongside Endurance.

Meanwhile, my reporter instincts were activated by political events. Argentina's ruling military junta saw the Ministry of Defence's recent decision to scrap Endurance as a sign of declining British interest in the region. Argentina had long claimed sovereignty over the Falkland Islands, leading the ship's captain, Nick Barker to forecast that an invasion was imminent. He had already alerted Whitehall to Argentine military activity and repeated those warnings in early 1982, hoping for naval reinforcements. But he was ignored.

Endurance was Falklands-bound when the April invasion came, but alone, with limited fire-power, couldn't have stopped it.

Britain's Task Force recaptured the islands and Endurance was reprieved from the MoD axe. However, being proved right was no satisfaction for Captain Barker. Up to his death in 1997 he insisted that the loss of more than 1,000 British and Argentine servicemen during the hostilities could have been avoided had his warnings been heeded, and action taken to head off the invasion.

It is particularly uplifting to see a Wood Warbler parachuting through fresh foliage and hear its resounding trill eclipsing other sounds.

OUT OF AN AFRICAN IMPASSE

Ian Wallace is the Grand Old Man of British Birding, with more than 60 years' experience under his belt. Of Scottish ancestry, he did his National Service in Kenya during the Mau Mau rebellion. Later, he spent three years in Nigeria.

On 1 March 1971, I finally had leave and could do the drive from Lagos to Lake Chad and back. With a Mercedes 200, driver Andrew, four cases of Star Lager, bins and a bird book, an adventure beckoned...

We came to the vale of the River Niger and stopped. I got out of the car, determined not to see the mighty Niger for the first time from a car seat. I left the road and pushed through the bush to reach the river. And then, there it was before me, wide, grey-blue and full of power. A photograph begged to be taken.

No sooner had I done so, than I was surrounded by soldiers, all pointing their semi-automatic rifles at me. I soon gathered that photographing the bridge was an offence under the rules of the Civil War. My Zeiss Contarex was taken but thanks to its fiendishly complicated opening system, they didn't expose the film.

Leaving me rooted to the spot by the meanest-looking private with the biggest rifle, the squad went in search of further counsel. An interesting shrike appeared but I dared not look. I heard Andrew being collected for questioning. Then, there were two happy coincidences. First, Andrew discovered two friends in the bridge guard. Then, a company sergeant major emerged from the thicket. He took in my Royal Scots bonnet and officer's badge and saluted. "Sorry about these ignorant fellows, sir. Come with me and we'll sort this out."

The CSM had been in the West African Frontier Force before Independence. The end of Empire was not quite complete. Calm, politeness and patience – and no show of angry panic – had won the day. Lubricated by Star beer, we all parted happily, my life 40 tense minutes shorter.

Redpolls are favourites of mine because they are small, charming, urgent beings that present all sorts of puzzles – certainly not boring!

ONE-HIT WONDER

Sheffield-born Chris Watson is an award-winning wildlife recordist who has worked with, among others, Sir David Attenborough and George Best. In his mis-spent youth he was a member of the experimental rock band Cabaret Voltaire. He is now a 'soft southerner' in Tyneside.

Speyside, the last week of April. My quest: to record the lekking of the Capercaillie. All I needed was an all-weather sleeping bag, a packet of biscuits, a hip flask filled with my favourite single malt…and about 15 kilos of recording equipment!

In the dark, I nearly walked straight past the 'hide', which was a fallen trunk draped with branches and brushwood. The lek was about 60 metres away, so my stereo mike cable snaked across the forest floor, and connected with two microphones hidden on the edge of the lek. I was holding my breath. Would the mikes work through the night? Would the weather hold? Would something eat through the cable?

I hardly slept. Just listening to the sounds of the forest around me was thrilling. Then, at 3.30 am, there was a huge rush of wings as a caper dropped onto the lek. Barely breathing, I tuned into the dry brush of feathers against the pine needles.

For over 50 minutes, I recorded one of the most spectacular displays I have ever heard from a bird. Massive wing flaps, followed by intimate 'champagne cork' clicks and pops which can only really be heard in extreme close-up. Eventually the bird moved off, the wing sounds gradually disappearing into the forest.

Over three nights in the forest – while the weather and my whisky held out – I made a remarkable collection of recordings which I eventually published on a CD. My caper track not only won an award at a festival held by an Austrian broadcast company…but the musician Bjork included it in a selection of her favourite pieces for Radio 3!

In spring, my favourite sound is the haunting song of the beautifully marked Golden Plover drifiting across the upland heather moors.

WITH THIS RING...

As founder and chairman of CJ Wildbird Foods, Chris Whittles is one of Britain's leading bird entrepreneurs. Trained as an agriculturalist, he is also a qualified bird ringer and founder member of the Northants Bird Club.

When I was a young, and a newly qualified 'C' ringer – the bottom of the heap – my trainer took me to catch a Spotted Crake that had been seen on some nearby brick pits.

Now the crake is normally an elusive bird, but when we arrived at the site, we saw our prey walk casually over the muddy surface of the pit, feeding as it went. Donning our wellies, and clutching mist net and poles, we too set off across the pit. The mud was soft and the going heavy, but we succeeded in erecting our net.

Our objective was to drive the bird into the net. On the first attempt, the crake emerged from the reeds and started to cross the pit, then, just as it reached the net, it took off and flew over it. We had to go to the other side and drive it back. Once again, the bird approached, but then flew around the net to the opposite side of the pit. On our third attempt, it walked underneath the net.

Meanwhile, every time we crossed the pit, the mud was becoming softer and wetter, and very soon, we were covered in the stuff! We decided to 'rush' the bird. As it walked from the edge of the reeds towards the net, we went for it – as much as we could in our heavy, mud-caked wellies.

Success! The crake hit the net and was caught at last. We struggled towards the net. The bird struggled in the net. We tripped over a sunken branch and fell headfirst into the thick mud of the pit. The bird tore the net and fell out, then walked calmly to the edge of the pit and took off, never to be seen again!

There is no more magnificent sight than thousands of Brambling fluttering over a winter feeding site.

LET ROBBIE WILLIAMS ENTERTAIN YOU!

His interest in birds started when Rob Williams saw a Sparrowhawk kill a Starling when he was three years old. Later, the frustration of land-locked birding in Somerset drove him to fantasies of more exotic birdwatching. He now lives in Ecuador and works as a conservation ecologist for BirdLife International.

Bird tours, especially those to far-flung corners of the world, are often marred by the participants' fears of 'dipping' – missing out on the bird of a lifetime. On one trip, to an obscure corner of South America, a pair of leather-clad listers became more and more driven by an obsession to see the rare and elusive Rufous-winged Ground Cuckoo. As other members of the group caught glimpses of the mythical bird, their frustration became desperate.

The two leaders tried to keep the situation under control, as the social harmony of the group began to disintegrate and members were on the verge of coming to blows.

Finally, a tripod-clubbing incident on a bridge at dusk, followed by an exchange of fists over the dinner table, signalled the irrevocable breakdown of the group.

The two social outcasts dropped out of the final day's birding, preferring to look for other birds alone. Justice was sweet: while they were drenched by pouring rain, had their lunch eaten by feral dogs, and failed to see any new birds, we had an unforgettable day's birding, culminating with sightings of such sought-after species as Giant Snipe and Bearded Tachuri, as the sun set over the tepuis.

This is a true morality tale: the contrast between the joy of birding together as a group and the destructive selfish obsession to which a few birders can occasionally be driven. Even today, many years later, I still shake with fear at its recollection.

Wherever you see a Long-eared Owl it is always special, but on moorland in the dawn light, floating through early morning mist, it's unforgettable.

DIVIDED BY A COMMON LANGUAGE

Stuart Winter is the only tabloid journalist in Britain to have his own columns about birdwatching as he writes both the Daily Star's *'Strictly for the Birds' and the* Sunday Express's *'Birdman of Blackfriars'. He lives in Luton, but his spiritual home is the USA.*

I had always been addicted to the American Dream – McDonalds, Tamla Motown, Pamela Anderson's swimsuit... and American birds. Now here I was, leaving Los Angeles in a sleek sports coupe, on my first US birding adventure.

A river mouth on the Pacific Ocean promised birds, and was soon serving them up with the enthusiasm of a diner waitress. Rafts of terns and waders stretched to the horizon, as pelicans plunged into the waves. I waded into the warm, clear waters.

My quest was a flock of 'peeps' – Western Sandpipers. They may not look exciting, but they are the ultimate identification challenge: several similar species only told apart by tiny plumage details. But these were so close that I could identify them with ease, just by their shape and structure.

A crocodile of American birders arrived, to be greeted with my animated lecture. "We Brits think these birds are really hard to put a name to," I explained. "But here you can identify them just on...well, jizz."

There was a long, drawn out pause. Faces frowned. Old ladies blushed. Then the leather-skinned leader drew breath and declared: "Shucks, I was told you Brits know their birds, but that sure takes some beatin', boy."

Shaking their heads, they headed off across the brackish waters, leaving a younger guy behind, the badges on his baseball cap singling him out as a seasoned traveller. He approached with a knowing smile, and whispered:

"A word of advice: on this side of the Pond, jissum is slang for semen!"

Elegant, dashing, the ultimate aerial hunter, the Hobby is not just a bird of prey but nature's finest defier of gravity.

STARTING YOUNG

Stephen Moss has been watching birds for as long as he can remember. He is a broadcaster, writer and very occasional twitcher, and has produced various BBC television series on birds and wildlife.

It all started with some funny black ducks. One winter's day in 1963, my mother drove me down to the river in her yellow Ford Anglia, to feed the birds. After chucking a few pieces of bread in their general direction, I turned to her and asked the question that would change my life. "What are those funny black ducks?"

Okay, so it isn't quite up to "why is the earth round?", or "are we alone in the universe?" But to be fair, I was only three years old. And to my mother's eternal credit, instead of changing the subject, she promised to find out.

At home, she dug out a copy of the *Observer's Book of Birds*, which someone had given me for Christmas. Glancing through its pages, we found the solution to the mystery: not 'funny black ducks' at all, but Coots.

From then on, I was well and truly hooked, my obsession fuelled by this little brown book. With all the tenacity of a young child, I proceeded to learn it more or less by heart, from the Magpie on the first page, to the Capercaillie on the last. I went on to watch birds wherever I went: first at the local gravel pit, then on family holidays, and finally all over the world, in every continent bar Australasia. Birding has become a lifelong obsession – rather like being a West Ham supporter, I suppose, but without so much agony and heartache.

And even now, every time I see a Coot amongst a flock of ducks, I say a silent prayer of thanks for the simple twist of fate that took me and my mother down to the riverbank, that dull winter's day more than 40 years ago.

My favourite bird is the Swift, because it is the ultimate flying machine, and the quintessential sound of the British summer!

SWAMPY

Robin Chittenden is a freelance wildlife photographer based in Norfolk. He is also the driving force behind Birdline East Anglia, which he set up in the late 1980s, and is a Photographic Researcher for British Birds *magazine. He is the photographer for this book.*

By its very nature, birding abroad takes you to remote places, where few tourists dare to tread. Naturally, the locals are often curious, which can at times become almost suffocating. In extreme cases, it can make birding almost impossible.

A few years ago, I was with my then girlfriend, Sarah, trying to photograph the gorgeous Kittlitz's Sand Plover in Egypt. Unfortunately, every time I attempted to stalk the bird, two locals hovering in the background would start to approach. This forced me to wander away, to avoid them inadvertently flushing the bird. Then, as they appeared to lose interest, I would again start to creep towards the plover.

This cat-and-mouse game went on for some time, but eventually I gave up and we drove off. An hour or so later, we returned, and to my great relief, the coast was clear. This time, with few distractions, I could concentrate completely on getting close to the bird. I crawled slowly towards it, using all my reserves of patience in order not to frighten it into taking flight. With all my attention completely focused on my quarry,

it was a while before I realized that I was sinking. The surface I was crawling over was no more than a

floating mass of swampy vegetation. If I did not take immediate action, I would sink into the water beneath, along with several thousand pounds worth of precious camera equipment!

I managed to escape a watery fate, but only just! When I had clawed my way back to solid ground, I suddenly realized that the persistent locals were only trying to warn me away from dangerous swampland!

Baillon's Crake is a strikingly beautifully marked and structured bird with the habitat of skulking in marshes well away from prying eyes.

EPILOGUE

So, there you have it: 40 blokes and 40 stories. But what are we to make of this diverse bunch of men and their tales?

For me, reading their accounts reminded me that birders are a paradoxical bunch. Forty individuals, drawn from all social and educational backgrounds, ages and ways of life, with as diverse a set of experiences as you could imagine. And yet they have something fundamental in common: the fact that birding gives their lives a structure and meaning increasingly hard to find in today's fragmented society.

Whether it is some genetic predisposition for appreciating the natural world that led them to watch birds; or a chance encounter with a bird that led to a curiosity about the natural world, I cannot tell.

What I do know is that birding enriches the quality of people's lives, and – perhaps uniquely – combines the competitiveness of sport, the aesthetics of art, the subliminal power of music, and the unpredictability of nature. So it is hardly surprising that for these forty men, and many other people around the world, it has become a lifetime's consuming passion.

Ultimately, the attraction of birds is founded on a paradox: that they are both familiar and accessible, yet beyond our control. As the great Canadian bird artist Robert Bateman wrote:

The lives of birds are elusive. They grace us with a few moments of beauty, then sail away on spaces of green and blue on voyages we will never take.

Stephen Moss

First published in 2003 by
New Holland Publishers (UK) Ltd
London • Cape Town • Sydney • Auckland
www.newhollandpublishers.com

Garfield House
86-88 Edgware Road
London W2 2EA
United Kingdom

80 McKenzie Street
Cape Town 8001
South Africa

Level 1, Unit 4
Suite 411, 14 Aquatic Drive
Frenchs Forest, NSW 2086
Australia

218 Lake Road
Northcote, Auckland
New Zealand

10 9 8 7 6 5 4 3

Editorial Direction: Jo Hemmings
Designer: Alan Marshall
Photographer: Robin Chittenden

Reproduction by Modern Age Repro House Ltd, Hong Kong
Printed and bound by Craft Print International Pte Ltd,
Singapore.

ISBN 1 84330 484 8

PHOTOGRAPHIC CREDITS:
Robin Chittenden: Cover – Spine, Back (All); pp 1–6;
8–10; 12–24; 26–31; 33; 35; 37; 39–45;
47–51; 53–54; 56–61; 63–67; 69–73; 75; 77–86; 88–93
Arnoud van den Berg: Cover – Front; p55
David Cottridge: pp 7; 76
ABTA (Phil Gammon): p25
Windrush Photography: pp 11; 32; 34; 36;
38; 46; 52; 62; 74
Paul Cook: p75
Anthony Wood: p95
Steve Young: p68
Anahi Plenge: p87

BY THE SAME AUTHOR:
Understanding Bird Behaviour; *How to Birdwatch*; *The Garden Bird Handbook* – all published by
New Holland.

The birdwatchers may be contacted via the Publishers.

Robin Chittenden may be contacted via:
Telephone: +44 0 (1) 603 633326,
Email: chittenden.robin@virgin.net
Internet at: www.birdnews.co.uk,
www.harlequinpictures.co.uk and
www.birdline-eastanglia.co.uk